# Selections for Colder Winters

Madison Roemer

BookLeaf Publishing

Presentation by *BookLeaf Publishing*

Web: www.bookleafpub.com

E-mail: info@bookleafpub.com


ISBN: 9789357616539

First edition 2022

*For Ike.*

# ACKNOWLEDGEMENT

It has been my general opinion that people who readily identify themselves as writers are an obnoxious sort, particularly if they do so right upon meeting a stranger. Therein lies the crux: when exactly does a relationship become close enough to divulge this predilection? It is due to this strange judgement that I owe my predicament: very few people in day-to-day life know that I am a writer. Perhaps they know that I edit- this I am readily able to claim that when asked how it is that I make my money. Maybe I've mentioned, briefly, that I freelance. Details are scant. I do not, in any circumstance, admit that I am writing fiction or poetry unless it is dragged out of me. In any case, then, I am very lucky to have an assortment of people who support me through my periods of unknowable, unseen, stress.

To my mother, first and foremost. She has read (very nearly) everything I have ever written, and to her credit we did not start off in the place we have reached. I am quite sure that the first inklings of me hoping to write started in her reading bedtime stories to me, which was long before I could read myself, and even further from the point where I would be putting together words so that I could read to her instead. Without her unending support I am sure I would have given up the entire idea many times over by now. The emotional composure to listen to a child tell you a story that you can hardly understand is a skill she must have been born with, as it is not one easily practiced.

I am still grateful for Kelly D. Holstine, who was- at one point- my English teacher, and is now the owner of WordHaven BookHouse in Sheboygan Wisconsin. Another early reader, Kelly endured several many youthful endeavors to put words together in a way that was "artistic"- and to these clumsy attempts I was granted only unending support and encouragement. Kelly, thank you. When the school year ended at last, I discovered that you were leaving and would not be my teacher the following year. I cried, despite always keeping my personal distance, and you told me that I impressed you every day. You told me never to stop writing. So I didn't. To you I owe my love of semicolons.

To the staff at Hidden Treasures thrift store, in Saint Anthony, Minnesota. You have all been such a wonderful support, even when you did not know what you were supporting. To Norma Jane, to Jens, to Nick- the management who let me organize and price books all day long- who let me work very strange early mornings so that I could go home to work on my mysterious projects. Thanks for never asking.

# PREFACE

I wrote all of the poems in this book (with the exception of one) in 2022. What was initially a poetic diary of frankly terrible poetry became the weed-filled garden from which I would pull (and edit) only my favorites to share with you.

What I never could have known when I set out on my, small, irreverent, quest, was that I would quite accidentally record the process of falling in love. If you do not enjoy love poetry, then I promise you that it will not hinder your enjoyment of this book. The process was actually quite painful. When I wrote the poems, too, I was mainly not aware that they were- indeed- love poems. Upon reading them back, however, I found that I was a love-drunk fool.

If you read very carefully this could read like a diary. If you don't read very carefully, you might enjoy it more.
Please take whatever feeling you can out of the poems in this book.
If you really do not like one, I invite you to tear it out and burn it (or chew it up, if you are particularly feral).

If you do not like the book at all, I request you donate it to a thrift store.

Thank you so very much for reading this book (or just any part of it), whether you bought it new, secondhand, or found it in a little library.

# Flower Prince

Twisting upward, branches dead
A crown of twining brambles atop his head-
Adorning tresses of chestnut hair,
Honed eyes locked in a stare.

For far off places,
Seen now only in dream-
For unrecognisable faces,
And all the things that could mean.

Atop a throne of well-placed words,
The Flower Prince of Metro Hope goes about his
day
Tongue pressed into his cheek, jokes unheard,
Winnows through and falls away.

A wild bloom,
A cheerful spirit,
Breathing room when you just can't hear it.
Half to be funny, half to be pretty-
Plastic flowers for a hint of pity.

# Birds

Light humming behind a tempest storm,
A flock of crows from a graveyard rising.
Beauty a fire that cannot keep us warm-
A squall becoming, metamorphosing.
O'er her soul call her "radiance",
But call her by her face.
No subtle hues or gradients,
You only name her grace.
But no more she the power to choose
The gentle turns of her countenance
Than the artist falls into his heart-found muse,
Despite his grinding doubtfulness.
There keep in mind this fact, o lovers:
The songbird ne'er asked for her colours.

# Whimper

Let it tangle up an image like a ball of string-
A painting of a feeling.
Let it sound of things you'd never sing-
All, in time, concealing.

A black and white video of a factory collapsing-
An atomic bomb,
Assigning words to static on an intercom.
A soundless record, and you write the words
Of great explosions; that you hear, but have
never been heard.

Imagining a cacophony-
The loudest sound ever heard-
Building and burning a fire to yet cinder.
A resonation of thunder!
A crack! A bellow burns tinder-!

And then the real sound meets your ear-
Hardly more than a whisper
Pull in closer, dear-
A vulnerable, scratchy, whimper.

# St. Mary's Orthodox

Fell no more trees and flowers;
Left gnarled, twining, root.
The surface sheared and clean now-
Untouched, the tangle underfoot.

Fell no more trees and flowers
And look at what you've wrought.
Be still your earthly powers;
Now mind the mass of rot.

Slow that filling of the pasture-
Now more than in the last year.

Barren land of sky and plot
Turned over a brand new hill of sod.

Fell no more trees and flowers
From our grasping human hands:
Strip bare to bone, tempest of time,
Even the strongest of our demands.

Though I grieve
And look to thee-
Mourn for them,
And not for me.

# Your Flame

A butane lighter from the side of the road
To light a candle in the hollow of her chest.
His gentle hand raised up against the world
To stop the wind from doing what wind does
best.
Have we faith in the flame to ignite,
Or in he to keep the wind at bay?
Have we faith in the lighter to light,
Or in her to keep alive the flame?
Now there they stand, at the mouth of the sea,
Barefooted she presents her heart for slaughter.
Will he bestow the candle back to me,
Or will he submerge it in the water?
Not ever was a soul prepared to pay such a price.
Yet never was a heart won without this sacrifice.

# Languish

She molders-
beckoned to return to the earth.
Artificially upkept
She ferments
Grows acrid to a dearth.

Poison now,
As poison becomes-
Venom now,
As softness succumbs.

Poison
As nightshade-
Poison as cyanide-
Poison that creeps slow and destroys from the
inside to the out.
Poison like arsenic- poison to drink and drink in
to drought.

Venom
Venomous like a wandering spider-
A bite that leaves no chance.
Venom like the black mamba
King cobra
The viper, Fer-de-lance

But dying just the same-
Bitter, wilting bloom,
A mantis with a head or two,
Searching for a groom.

# Besotted

In the throes
Of a skipping stone-
Mid go-about of a rock being thrown.

Reaching for a feeling like
Snowflakes in a flurry-
Each one more complicated than a single earthly
worry.

But I'm besotted
Taken
With a single grain of sand-
A single bolt of lightning-
A single work-worn hand.

The stone skipping,
A few seconds ticking-
Before it's rapidly sinking.

# Converging

O, of one hundred gilded things
I think only of mine.
Though the others be as fine-
Have I all of this endless time to think only of
this one.

Aye, of thirty springs
I will only taste of one-
Only bathe of one-
Only see the sun's fine rays glimmering off of
this one.

Of all the wonders my Lord will bring-
And options given me-
All the many seemingly free-
I know that it can only be that I would want this
one.

# Snow Days

There is a song
That has been put on
During the first snow
Each year, for as far back as my memory will
go.

I don't know
Exactly when
It changed from my father to me-
But like clockwork,
If that is how clocks worked-
Someone sets it carefully.

This year I remembered it,
Seven AM,
When the world is still black as coal.
When you were driving
Through a flurry of the first cursed chips of sky,
To the place where I worked.

And I put it on the car radio.

We sat in silence
And I said to you
That I've listened to this every year for

The full of my memory.
And I watched you listen to it with fresh ears,
As you drove on an empty freeway.

We didn't say a word for awhile after that,
But watched the twiling blue,
Take up on fresh caps of white.
And at a stoplight
I looked at you,
And you took a breath.

You had been alone for the holidays
Every year
For a near decade, then, you said.
But this year will be different.
The song ends.
And I realise I have been alone, too.

# Brothers

Your blue-eyed saviour
Has met my middle eastern man.

It is every couple,
Or ever few, months
That they get together and have coffee.

They get together and agree,
Nodding gently,
Each one letting the other speak.

They do not speak in unison,
Like twins in an old horror flick,
But they rarely disagree
On anything but semantics.

Yours, with a soft turn of a golden curl,
Explains how oft he is asked to drive a motor
vehicle,
And mine
Still rides a donkey.

# Death on a Cold January Morning

There is no weapon more powerful
Than human ego.
You probably would have agreed-
Cruel and yet markedly naive-
To how regular you are,
How ordinary the bad seed.

Yours was the first
I'd ever heard the phrase
"Emergency Divorce"-
That your own
Vileness
Was such a force-
Not a power like the one you had secretly
wielded,
But one thrust onto perfect strangers,
And used solely to remove your family
From humble dangers.

Like being associated with you
-which is a thing they have to do-
Of being carried through the legal proceedings
of a parade
Made to make us feel better

That we had ever let a man like you exist.
Simple profiling works like this:

You would be a white man.
In his twenties at the commission of the first.
Military background.
And feeling-
In some way or another-
Wronged by your mother.

Ordinary, predictable,
You followed the unwritten rules of your clade-
How banal it all seemed,
To the letter,
This terror that you'd made.

They could sell men like you in a box set.

# The Bridle

Bite down
The Bridle-
Baby in bassinet.
Carry down
The body-
Mouth wrapped 'round a cigarette.

Stare down
Your father-in-law.
He's asking you a question.
If words have meaning,
And he is talking,
Then why is he making no impression?

And now you wear no expression-
And as if by magic-
You suddenly hear his narration.
He is speaking.
Speaking.
Speaking.
About hell, about damnation.

You lean your weight against the wall-
This is all too heavy.
Mentally, maybe, but you'll get to forget.

Right then you just need to
Extinguish
That
Cigarette.

# Natural Order

Be I chevrotain
Or be I plover-
Must I dine on refuse
Or on bits of spry clover?

Call a man a symbiote
As he shows his teeth-
Or call a girl a synergist
For keeping them all clean.

Am I 'rarely photographed'
If I dine alone?
Nearly extinct and then
Neck exposed, and prone?

And what if I, too,
Had teeth to bare?

# Loveless Marriage I

He changes the showerhead back down
She drinks her milk whole-
Neither one seeing the signs of control.

His shirts are still mended,
He waters her plants,
And when she goes shopping
She picks out his pants.

On the third of the month,
He has a bad day.
He doesn't speak a word of it to her,
She wouldn't know what to say.

But also
He knows
It would still trouble her some,
To think of him struggling.
He's drumming his thumbs.

If only she would ask him
"How was your day?"
And then she does it
And he doesn't even say.

But later that night
She folds up his socks.
And come daylight savings
He changes the clocks.

A loveless marriage,
The both report,
But he's still wearing slacks
A little bit too short.

# Loveless Marriage II

Believe
That once you've smoked in a house
That the smell stays in the walls.

That there is a reason we raze homes
Where murderers kept their bones.

That cell towers feel
All your personal calls.

I think that you've grown a forest,
I think that you've tended those trees.
I also believe
That you burnt it all to the ground-
Flat-
And that you promise you've got no qualms
with that.

There's something you must know about forest
fire.
It creates fertiliser.
And now fresh green things come springing up
like new desire.

There must be a reason

We call passion a flame-
So dance in the ashes
And choose a new name.

# Black Flag

Up until now, I thought the whole of love
Was hard. I thought there would be sacrifice,
And that the pains were
Normal- like I would writhe free of my cocoon,
Shed it forcefully.

"Relationships are a lot of work."
It makes sense. I had dug up
From the ground as if had been seven years of
hard slumber-
And I needed to come up and die.

Now I,
The willing fly,
Saw your gentle web.
But the moment you saw me there you
Set me free.

I wanted,
It seemed,
To be splattered to pulp
On the windshield of your car.
This is how humans earn their love
But you wouldn't let me go that far.

And when I insisted I soon must change-
My metamorphosis-
You insisted that you like
What I was
Exactly equal to what I would become.
I didn't have to writhe-
I would just slip
Free into something else,
Without even noticing,
Until I found the need

And saw that I already had the wings.

# Eventide

Blows like chaff
And freshly
Comes up new
Like it wasn't all filthy just before.

Strange to think
Children in the mud
Get clean.
And the same way,
People mired in mistakes
Can wash them off.

With Christ
Or a very hot bath
Or a good honest apology
Or an intent to do better-
Be better-
Change.

Not like trees change, where we know they'll
either change back-
Or die.
Change like the hands of an old man
Get more and more gnarled
With love.

Time turns them into something else
And it does not change them back.

I want to change that way
If nothing more
Than to be new
To be different
And never to be this same thing again.

Not because there's anything wrong with this,
But because
I'm afraid I'll hold onto it forever
And always change back,
Like autumn colours,
Until the leaves don't grow back in,
And the city has to come cut me down.

# One or the Next

I hope God forgives you
The transgressions
He made it impossible
For mortal men to forget.

For never have I heard a soul
Utter
"I believe in second chances"
Without knowing them well enough-
Within those first few glances-
To see if it is for themselves they ask
Or if
They might love someone who has a disaster in
their past.

# Hunting for Sport

On a pilgrimage,
Drunk with foliage,
Surrounded, in full, by the world's raw bones.
New life springing from spots of ground not
glimpsed in a century-
Moss growing from clefts in the stones.

Sickly sweet swell of earthen sacrifice-
Here at the exposed neck of the world-
Every stillness face to him,
And leaves with flowers unfurled.

A lone traveller marches
Forward, deftly,
Goes blindly in the dark.
Thinking surely,

'Curtail until curtain
If you'd like to miss your mark-
All arrows left in quiver,
Quicker-
Forego the starting spark.'

But blood in open waters
Nearly always

Draws a shark.

He is no longer alone now,
God has spoken up a fawn.
He chose the spot at eventide and now there is
abundant dawn.

Hinds' Feet in low places,
Gentle head in lull,
A dewdrop fed puddle
is taken in in full.

And behind it in the tree line,
He cannot believe his luck,
The spirit of this forest,
A broad-built, aged, buck.

How is it that a man could be
Steeped in all the greenery-
Bathed
in all that God has made-
Welcomed to be hewn within the scenery-

And still
Found no simple beauty-
Human parts undone-
Viewed all these things alone,
And still went for his gun.

# Mixing Paints

The painter stands
In a field of flowers
Mixing up his paints.

There he will dawdle for several hours,
Loosening all his restraints.

And when he is ready
He will take up his brush
And begin to move colours of auburn and blush

As the oar moves the water
Or a slow moving stream
Moves light and due colour
Where colour should be

Guided by God
Or by fact
Or by science-
Stricken, in fact, by his own "self-reliance",
The painter is puppeted to draw out the scene
Exactly as his eyes take it to mean.

And a viewer may ask
'Sir, I beg your pardon,

Which is the art?
The painting
Or the garden?'

# Art's a Bug on my Windshield

You're moving much too fast
No seatbelt,
Picasso.

You say you're built to last
Heart melts,
Picasso.

You've been slamming puzzles together to make
Your own Picasso.
And they don't know who you are.

Shelley's chimera,
Darwin's best-
Variegated monstera-
Most desired guest.

Who would have thought that a stream of
accidents
Could be an artist?
Picasso:
Divine spread of glass on a sidewalk.